LIVING IN THE READER'S WORLD

ADULT BASIC EDUCATION

Book 2

CAMBRIDGE
THE ADULT EDUCATION COMPANY
888 Seventh Avenue New York, N.Y. 10106

LIVING
in the Reader's World

Executive Editor: Brian Schenk

Project Editor: Dennis Mendyk

Contributing Editor: Laura Daly

ISBN   0–8428–9515–9

9   8   7   6   5   4   3

CONTENTS

INSTRUCTIONS

Unit 1   (Looking at Instructions)   1

Unit 2   (Looking at Steps in Instructions)   11

Unit 3   (Using Headings to Find Instructions)   20

Unit 4   (Review)   32

Unit 5   (Using a Table of Contents to
                  Find Instructions)   37

Unit 6   (Using Pictures to Understand Instructions)   48

Unit 7   (Using Clues to Understand Unfamiliar Words)   60

Unit 8   (Review)   69

NEWSPAPERS

Unit 9   (Looking at a Newspaper's Index)   77

Unit 10   (Looking at Headlines)   88

Unit 11   (Using Clues to Understand a Headline)   96

Unit 12   (Review)   107

Unit 13   (Reading Longer Sentences)   114

Unit 14   (Using Clues to Understand Unfamiliar Words)   127

Unit 15   (Final Review)   137

APPENDIX: Unit Outlines and Word Lists   147

IMPORTANT NOTE TO THE INSTRUCTOR

Please read the appendix to this book before you begin any instruction. The appendix begins on page 147.

UNIT 1

Suppose you are driving down a road.

You see some road signs as you drive.

Most of the signs tell you to do something.

STOP!   KEEP RIGHT!   YIELD!

Or they tell you <u>not</u> to do something.

NO PARKING!   NO LEFT TURN!   DO NOT ENTER!

1

Now suppose you go to a store.

A lot of signs in the store will tell you to do something.

The sign on the door may say PUSH or PULL.

Ads in the store tell you to buy things.

Some of the signs tell you <u>not</u> to do something.

There may be a sign that says NO SMOKING.

Or there may be a sign that says NO PETS.

———————

Many signs tell you to do something.

They give you <u>instructions</u>.

A lot of things that you read are instructions.

For example, think about this.

Suppose you have a headache.

You want to take some aspirin.

You get a bottle of aspirin.

How do you open it?

TO OPEN:
LINE UP ARROWS
ON CAP & BOTTLE.
PUSH CAP UP
WITH THUMB.

The instructions tell you how to open the bottle.

They make it easy for you to use the aspirin.

———————

Here are some other instructions.

They are on the bottle's label.

DOSAGE:

For adults: Take 1 to 2 tablets every 4 hours.

For children   (ages 10 to 15):   Take 1 tablet every 4 hours.
                       (ages 5 to 10):   Take $\frac{1}{2}$ tablet every 4 hours.
                       (ages 3 to 5):   Take $\frac{1}{4}$ tablet every 4 hours.

For children younger than 3:   Call your doctor.

WARNING: KEEP OUT OF REACH OF CHILDREN.

These instructions help you to use the aspirin safely.

They tell you how many tablets to take.

And they tell you to keep the aspirin in a safe place.

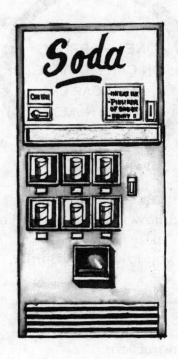

Suppose you are in a bus station.

You're waiting for a bus.

You want to have something to drink.

There is a soda machine in the bus station.

How would you buy some soda from the machine?

You could buy some soda by putting money in the machine.

But how would you know how much money to put in?

4

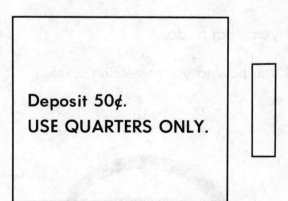

Deposit 50¢.
USE QUARTERS ONLY.

You would look at the instructions on the machine.

The instructions tell you how to get soda from the machine.

They tell you how much money a soda costs.

How much money would you need to get a soda from this machine?

What kind of money would you need?

A lot of things that you read are instructions.

Instructions may tell you how something works.

They may tell you what to do.

They may tell you how to use something safely.

TO OPEN:
LINE UP ARROWS
ON CAP & BOTTLE.
PUSH CAP UP
WITH THUMB.

Deposit 50¢.
USE QUARTERS ONLY.

TRYING IT OUT

Look at the instructions.

Then answer the questions about them.

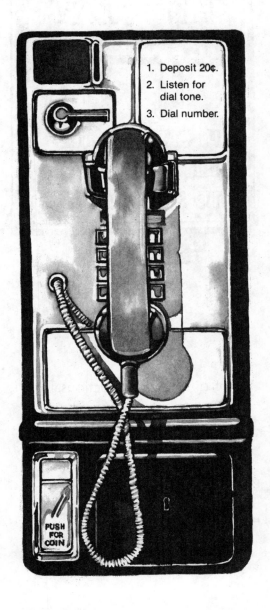

1. Deposit 20¢.
2. Listen for dial tone.
3. Dial number.

PUSH FOR COIN

What are these instructions for?

What do they tell you?

What are these instructions for?

When should you use the alarm?

PUTTING WORDS IN THEIR PLACE

Fill in the blanks.

Use the words in the list.

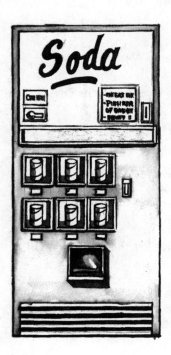

on the machine

a soda machine

from the machine

in the machine

This is —————————————.

The soda is —————————————.

The instructions are —————————————.

They tell you how to buy soda —————————————.

LOOKING AT WORDS

Here is a line from page 4:

You're waiting for a bus.

You're stands for "you are."

You're is a short way to say "you are."

Look at the underlined words below.

What do the words stand for?

There's a soda machine in the bus station.

But it doesn't work.

There isn't any soda in it.

It's empty.

TRYING IT ON YOUR OWN

Look for instructions on a machine.

Do the instructions tell you how to use the machine?

Do they tell you any other things?

UNIT 2

Here are some instructions.

They tell you how to use a pay phone.

1. Deposit 20¢.

2. Listen for
   dial tone.

3. Dial number.

Each line in the instructions has a number.

What do the numbers stand for?

```
1.  Deposit 20¢.

2.  Listen for
    dial tone.

3.  Dial number.
```

The numbers stand for steps.

They tell you the order of the instructions.

To use the phone, you have to follow the steps in their right
    order.

First you deposit 20¢ into the phone.

Then you listen for the dial tone.

Then you dial the number.

Here are instructions from a soda machine.

- Deposit 50¢.
- Press button for soda desired.
- If soda does not appear, press button again.
- If soda still does not appear, press another button.

There aren't any numbers in the instructions.

But the steps are put in order.

You have to follow the order to use the machine.

First you have to put the money in the machine.

Then you press the button to get a soda.

Here are some more instructions.

They are for opening an aspirin bottle.

TO OPEN:
LINE UP ARROWS
ON CAP & BOTTLE.
PUSH CAP UP
WITH THUMB.

What is the first step to open the bottle?

What is the next step?

What do you think would happen if you didn't do the first step?

Many instructions are given in steps.

Most of the time, the steps are in order.

To follow the instructions, you have to follow the order of the
steps.

1. Deposit 20¢.

2. Listen for
   dial tone.

3. Dial number.

TO OPEN:
LINE UP ARROWS
ON CAP & BOTTLE.
PUSH CAP UP
WITH THUMB.

TRYING IT OUT

Look at the instructions.

Then answer the questions about them.

FUD'S SODA
$25,000 GIVEAWAY

To enter:
1. Fill in the form below with your name, address, and phone number.
2. On the bottom line, tell us why you like Fud's soda.
3. Send the form to:
   FUD'S GIVEAWAY
   282 North Road
   North Town, OH
4. Send the form before June 30.

Name _____

Address _____

_____

Phone _____

Why I like Fud's: _____

_____

---

1. What is this ad about?

2. What are the instructions for?

3. Is there a heading to tell you where the instructions are?

4. In your own words, tell what the instructions are.

```
+------------------------------------------+
|                  OK                      |
|            Chicken Soup                  |
|                                          |
|                                          |
|   Directions:                            |
|   ‾‾‾‾‾‾‾‾‾‾                              |
|                                          |
|   1.   Empty soup into pot.              |
|   2.   Add 1 can of water to soup.       |
|   3.   Heat soup until boiling.          |
|                                          |
+------------------------------------------+
```

1.   What are these instructions for?

2.   How many steps are in the instructions?

3.   Are the steps in order?
     How can you tell?

PUTTING WORDS IN THEIR PLACE

Fill in the blanks.

Use the words in the list.

---

1. Deposit 20¢.

2. Listen for dial tone.

3. Dial number.

---

into the phone
for the dial tone
from a pay phone
the number
in the instructions

These instructions are —————————————.

To use the phone, you follow the steps —————————————.

First you deposit 20¢ —————————————.

Then you listen —————————————.

Then you dial —————————————.

LOOKING AT WORDS

You looked at these two words on page 14:

open   opening

The two words are almost the same.

The second word has "open" in it.

But it has another part added to it.

Look at each underlined word below.

Do you know any of the parts in the word?

Can you tell what the word is?

I deposited 20¢ into the pay phone.

I listened for the dial tone.

I started dialing the number.

But nothing happened.

The phone wasn't working.

TRY IT ON YOUR OWN

Look for instructions on a can of food.

Do the instructions have a heading?

Are the instructions given in order?

UNIT 3

Suppose you want to make something to eat.

You have a can of soup.

Suppose you've never made soup before.

You need instructions on how to make the soup.

Where would you find the instructions?

```
┌─────────────────────────────────────────────┐
│                                             │
│                    OK                       │
│               Chicken Soup                  │
│              _____                │
│                                             │
│                                             │
│   INGREDIENTS:   Chicken stock, chicken fat,│
│      salt, chicken, preservatives           │
│                                             │
│                                             │
│   SERVING INFORMATION:                      │
│                                             │
│      serving size:   12 oz.                 │
│      number of servings:   2                │
│      calories:   240                        │
│                                             │
│                                             │
│   DIRECTIONS:                               │
│                                             │
│   1.  Empty soup into pot.                  │
│   2.  Add 1 can of water to soup.           │
│   3.  Heat soup until boiling.              │
│                                             │
└─────────────────────────────────────────────┘
```

You would look at the label.

The instructions are on the label.

But other things are also listed on the label.

How would you find the instructions?

OK
Chicken Soup

INGREDIENTS: Chicken stock, chicken fat, salt, chicken, preservatives

SERVING INFORMATION:

serving size: 12 oz.
number of servings: 2
calories: 240

DIRECTIONS:

1. Empty soup into pot.
2. Add 1 can of water to soup.
3. Heat soup until boiling.

You could look at the headings.

The headings tell you what is listed.

Look at the headings on the label.

Which heading is for the instructions?

The first heading is "Ingredients."

"Ingredients" are the things that are in the soup.

The second heading is "Serving Information."

"Serving Information" tells you other things about the soup.

The third heading is "Directions."

"Directions" tell you how to make the soup.

"Directions" are instructions.

Headings make things easier to find.

They tell you what things are.

Most instructions have headings.

But some don't.

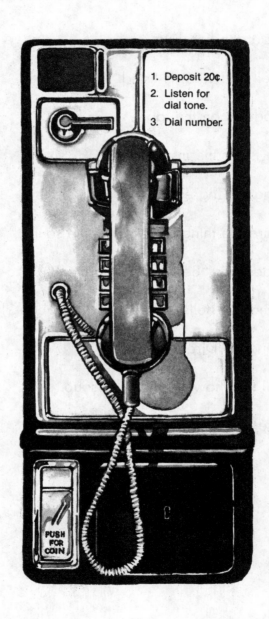

```
1.  Deposit 20¢.

2.  Listen for
    dial tone.

3.  Dial number.
```

These instructions don't have a heading.

They don't need a heading.

They are right next to the coin slot on a pay phone.

But suppose you want to make a long-distance phone call.

Are there any other instructions to help you?

Credit card calls Collect calls	Dial 0 + Area Code + Number
Long-distance calls	Dial 1 + Area Code + Number
Toll-free (800) calls	Dial 1 + 800 + Number
Directory assistance	Dial 411 Dial 1 + Area Code + 555-1212 for long-distance assistance

This is a long list of instructions on the phone.

These instructions tell you how to make special calls.

How would you find the instructions for a long-distance call?

Would you have to read all the instructions?

You don't have to read all the instructions.

You can find the right instructions by looking at the headings.

Look down the list of headings.

Find the heading for long-distance phone calls.

Then read the instructions for making a long-distance call.

Many instructions have headings on them.

The headings tell what the instructions are.

They help to make instructions easier to find.

TRYING IT OUT

Here are instructions from a pay phone.

Use the headings to answer the questions about the instructions.

Credit card calls Collect calls	Dial 0 + Area Code + Number
Long-distance calls	Dial 1 + Area Code + Number
Toll-free (800) calls	Dial 1 + 800 + Number
Directory assistance	Dial 411 Dial 1 + Area Code + 555-1212 for long-distance assistance

1. You want to dial a long-distance call.

   How do you do it?

2. You want to make a collect phone call.

   What number do you dial?

3. You want to make a long-distance call.

   But you don't have the phone number.

   Is there a number you can dial for help?

   What is the number?

PUTTING WORDS IN THEIR PLACE

Fill in the blanks.

Use the words in the list.

```
OK
Chicken Soup


Directions:


1.  Empty soup into pot.
2.  Add 1 can of water to soup.
3.  Heat soup until boiling.
```

made

to make

can make

making

These instructions are for _____ soup.

The instructions tell you how _____ soup.

The instructions can help you if you have never _____ soup.

If you follow the instructions, you _____ soup.

LOOKING AT WORDS

Read the lines below.

Look at the underlined words.

Can you tell what the words are?

I found a can of soup.

I emptied the soup into a pot.

I added a can of water to the soup.

I heated the soup.

Then I had some of the soup.

I didn't like it.

UNIT 4   (REVIEW)

Look at this ad.

Then answer the questions about it on the next page.

How can YOU win $50,000?

IT'S EASY!

All you have to do is enter the

OK FOOD
COMPANY'S
LABEL CONTEST

Here's how to enter:

- Buy any OK food.
- Put your name and address on the back of the label.
- Send the label to:
  OK CONTEST
  Box 4957
  Watertown, NC

1. What is this ad about?

2. What are the instructions in the ad for?

3. Are the instructions put in order?

4. What is the address in the instructions for?

5. Suppose you buy a can of OK chicken soup.

   What would you have to do to enter the contest?

Look at this label.

Then answer the questions about it.

1. Where are the instructions on this label?

2. How many steps are in the instructions?

3. Are the steps in order?

4. What are the steps?

Fill in the blanks.

Use the words in the list.

DOSAGE:

For adults: Take 1 to 2 tablets every 4 hours.

For children   (ages 10 to 15):   Take 1 tablet every 4 hours.
               (ages 5 to 10):   Take $\frac{1}{2}$ tablet every 4 hours.
               (ages 3 to 5):   Take $\frac{1}{4}$ tablet every 4 hours.

For children younger than 3:   Call your doctor.

WARNING: KEEP OUT OF REACH OF CHILDREN.

---

on

from

in

of

These instructions are _____ an aspirin bottle.

The instructions are printed _____ the bottle's label.

The instructions tell you the number _____ tablets to take.

They tell you to keep the aspirin _____ a safe place.

Read each line below.

Look at the <u>underlined</u> words.

Can you tell what the underlined words stand for?

I have a can of soup.

But I <u>can't</u> use it.

<u>There's</u> no label on it.

There <u>aren't</u> any instructions on it.

I <u>don't</u> know how to make soup.

UNIT 5

Suppose you want to buy a new coffee maker.

You see one that is on sale.

You have never used this kind of coffee maker before.

But it is a good buy, so you buy it.

You take your new coffee maker home.

You want to try it out.

But you need instructions on how to use it.

You open the box.

There's a booklet inside the box.

YOUR NEW COFFEE MAKER

The booklet tells you everything about your new machine.

But you don't want to know everything.

You only want to know how to use it.

There are a lot of pages in the booklet.

How can you find the instructions in the booklet?

TABLE OF CONTENTS

About your coffee maker .... page 3

How to use your coffee maker .... page 6

How to clean your coffee maker .... page 8

How to get new parts for your

coffee maker .... page 11

Warranty information .... page 12

You can look at the <u>table of contents.</u>

The table of contents is a list of headings.

There is a page number next to each heading.

The page number tells you where to find the information you
need.

Look down the list of headings.

Where would you find the instructions for using the coffee maker?

The instructions are on page 6.

They are listed under the heading "HOW TO USE YOUR COFFEE MAKER."

HOW TO USE YOUR COFFEE MAKER

1. Place filter into holder.
2. Put coffee into holder. Use 5 scoops of coffee for a full pot of coffee.
3. Slide the holder into its slot at the top of the coffee maker.
4. Fill the glass pot with <u>cold</u> water.
5. Pour the water into the hole at the top of the coffee maker. Plug in the coffee maker.
6. Place the glass pot under the holder. Turn the switch to "brew."

Your coffee will be ready in 3 minutes!

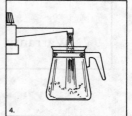

Look at the instructions.

There are two parts in the instructions.

The first part is the list of steps.

The steps tell you how to use the coffee maker.

The second part is a set of pictures.

The pictures show you how to use the coffee maker.

They help to make the steps easier to follow.

Each step has a picture.

Look at the picture for step 1.

It shows you the filter and the holder.

You don't have to guess what the filter and holder look like.

You have looked at two things in this unit.

First, you looked at a table of contents.

A table of contents is a list of headings.

Many booklets have a table of contents.

You have to use the table of contents to find information in a booklet.

Second, you looked at pictures in instructions.

Some instructions come with pictures.

The pictures make the instructions easier to follow.

The pictures show you the steps in the instructions.

You can use the pictures to understand the steps better.

TRYING IT OUT

Answer the questions about the table of contents.

TABLE OF CONTENTS

About your coffee maker .... page 3
How to use your coffee maker .... page 6
How to clean your coffee maker .... page 8
How to get new parts for your
                coffee maker .... page 11
Warranty information .... page 12

1. You want to find out how to clean the coffee maker.

   What page should you turn to?

2. You need a new glass pot for your coffee maker.

   Does the booklet tell you where to get a new pot?

3. What is on page 3?

   What do you think the information on page 3 will tell you?

Answer the questions about these instructions.

The questions are on page 45.

HOW TO USE YOUR COFFEE MAKER

1. Place filter into holder.
2. Put coffee into holder. Use 5 scoops of coffee for a full pot of coffee.
3. Slide the holder into its slot at the top of the coffee maker.
4. Fill the glass pot with <u>cold</u> water.
5. Pour the water into the hole at the top of the coffee maker. Plug in the coffee maker.
6. Place the glass pot under the holder. Turn the switch to "brew."

Your coffee will be ready in 3 minutes!

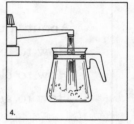

1. You want to make a full pot of coffee.

   How much coffee should you put in the holder?

   What step tells you this?

2. What kind of water should you use in the coffee maker?

   What step tells you this?

3. Read step 6.

   Then look at the picture for step 6.

   Where is the "brew" switch for the coffee maker?

   How can you tell?

4. You have followed all 6 steps.

   How long will it take to brew the coffee?

   How do you know?

PUTTING WORDS IN THEIR PLACE

Fill in the blanks.

TABLE OF CONTENTS

About your coffee maker .... page 3

How to use your coffee maker .... page 6

How to clean your coffee maker .... page 8

How to get new parts for your

                         coffee maker .... page 11

Warranty information .... page 12

This is a table of contents.

A table of _____ is a list _____ headings.

There is _____ page number next _____ each

    heading.

The _____ number tells you _____ to find the

    _____ you need.

LOOKING AT WORDS

You looked at these words in this unit:

> inside   everything

Each word is made up of two short words.

> <u>in</u> + <u>side</u> ⟶ <u>inside</u>
>
> <u>every</u> + <u>thing</u> ⟶ <u>everything</u>

Read each line below.

Look at the <u>underlined</u> words.

Can you see the two words in the underlined word?

I found a box <u>outside</u> my house.

<u>However</u>, there wasn't <u>anything</u> in it.

<u>Someday</u>, I'll find a box with <u>something</u> in it.

<u>Whatever</u> it is, I hope it's good.

TRY IT ON YOUR OWN

Find an instruction booklet.

Does it have a table of contents?

Do the instructions come with pictures?

UNIT 6

A smoke alarm is something you can put in your home.

The alarm goes off if there is smoke in the air.

A lot of people think smoke alarms are a good idea.

They think smoke alarms can save lives.

Suppose you got a smoke alarm.

What would you do with it?

How would you get it to work?

You can find out more about the smoke alarm by looking at the instructions.

The instructions tell you about the smoke alarm.

They tell you where the smoke alarm should go.

They tell you how to put the smoke alarm in place.

They tell you how to get the smoke alarm to work.

THE
LIFE
SAVER

SMOKE ALARM

Look at these instructions.

TESTING YOUR NEW SMOKE ALARM

Here's how to test your new smoke alarm to see if it works.
First, get a 9-volt battery. Put it in place in the battery
holder. The battery holder is at the back of the smoke
alarm.

When the battery is in place, the alarm is ready be
tested. To test the alarm, press the <u>test button</u>. The test
button is on the front of the alarm. Hold the test button
down for 5–10 seconds. The alarm should go off.

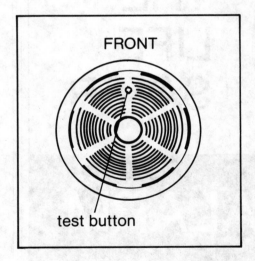
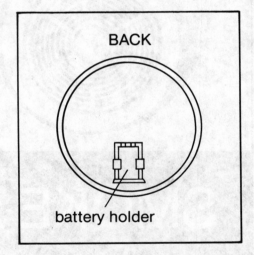

FRONT

test button

BACK

battery holder

If the alarm does not go off, try another 9-volt battery. If the
alarm still does not go off, return the alarm to the store.
It may be defective.

The heading tells you what the instructions are for.

The instructions tell you how to test the smoke alarm.

Look at the pictures in the instructions.

What do they show you?

The first picture shows the front of the smoke alarm.

The second picture shows the back of the smoke alarm.

What do the lines in the pictures point to?

How can you tell?

Here are some more instructions for the smoke alarm.

SETTING UP YOUR NEW SMOKE ALARM

You can put your smoke alarm in place in two easy steps.

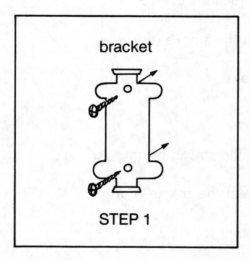

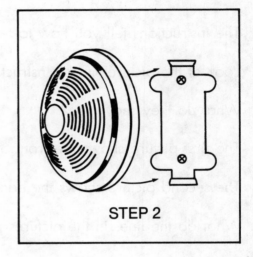

1. Hold the bracket in place on the wall or ceiling.
    Use the two screws to attach the bracket to the wall or
    ceiling.

2. Snap the smoke alarm onto the bracket.

What are the instructions for?

How can you tell?

Look at the two pictures in the instructions.

What do the pictures show you?

————————

These instructions tell you how to set up the alarm.

The heading tells you this.

There are two steps to follow.

Each picture shows a step.

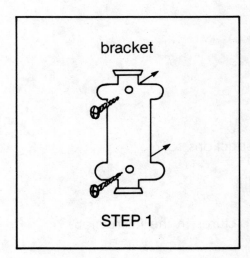

bracket

STEP 1

Here is the first step from the instructions.

Suppose you didn't know what a bracket looked like.

Does the picture help you?

The picture shows you the bracket.

It also shows you the two screws.

The arrows show you where the screws go.

The picture gives you a clearer idea about Step 1.

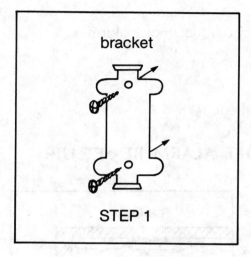

bracket

STEP 1

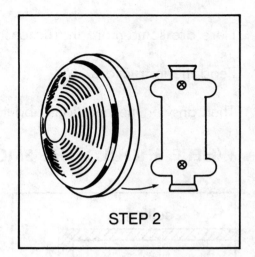

STEP 2

Pictures are often used in instructions.

They can help to make the instructions clearer.

Sometimes words are used in pictures.

The words point to things that you may not know.

These words also make the instructions clearer.

TRYING IT OUT

Here are some more instructions about the smoke alarm.

Read the instructions.

Then answer the questions about them.

WHERE SHOULD THE SMOKE ALARM BE SET UP?

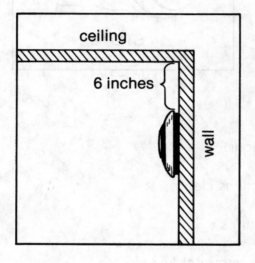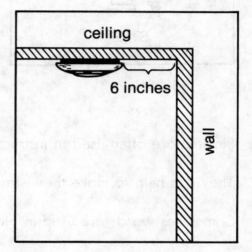

1. If you put the alarm on a wall, place it 6 inches from the ceiling.

2. If you put the alarm on the ceiling, place it at least 6 inches from the wall.

1. What are these instructions for?

2. What do the pictures show?

3. Do you think the pictures make the instructions clearer?

WHERE IS THE BEST PLACE TO PUT A SMOKE ALARM?

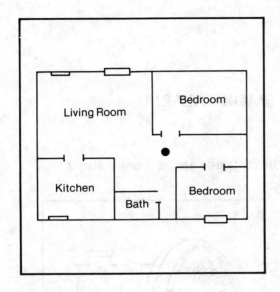 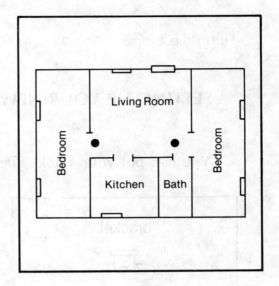

• smoke alarms

Always put the smoke alarm near the bedroom area.
If you have two bedroom areas, you should have two
   smoke alarms.

1. What do these instructions tell you?

2. What do the pictures show?

3. Look at the dots in the pictures.

   What do the dots stand for?

   How can you tell?

PUTTING WORDS IN THEIR PLACE

Fill in the blanks.

SETTING UP YOUR NEW SMOKE ALARM

You can put your smoke alarm in place in two easy steps.

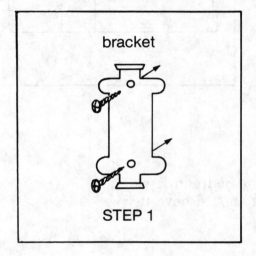

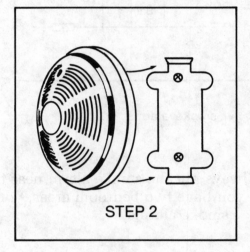

1. Hold the bracket in place on the wall or ceiling.
    Use the two screws to attach the bracket to the wall or
    ceiling.

2. Snap the smoke alarm onto the bracket.

These are some instructions for a smoke alarm.

They tell you _____ to set up the _____ .

There are _____ steps to set _____ the alarm.

The _____ show you the _____ steps.

The words _____ you about the _____ .

LOOKING AT WORDS

You looked at these two words in this unit:

save   sav<u>er</u>

Read the lines below.

Look at the <u>underlined</u> words.

Look for a word that you know.

Can you tell what the underlined words are?

Al is looking for work.

He says he is a good <u>worker</u>.

He says he is a fast <u>thinker</u>.

He used to be a <u>boxer</u>.

Now he wants to be a <u>waiter</u>.

TRY IT ON YOUR OWN

Look for pictures in instructions that have words in them.

Do the words make the pictures easier to understand?

UNIT 7

Look at these instructions.
They are for a toaster oven.

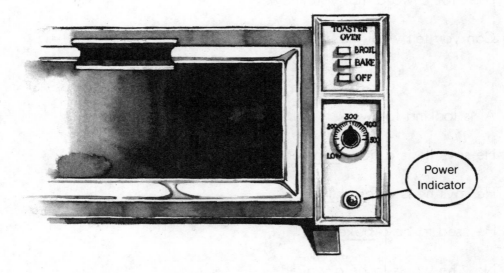

Your toaster oven comes with a power indicator.
The power indicator is a small light. When the
toaster oven is on, the power indicator lights up.
The power indicator will help you to use the toaster
oven safely. It will tell you when the toaster oven is on.

You may never have seen the words "power indicator" before.

But can you tell what a "power indicator" is?

Are there any clues in the instructions?

The first clue is in the picture.

The words "power indicator" are in the picture.

They show what the power indicator looks like.

They show where it is.

The second clue is in the instructions.

The instructions tell you about the power indicator.

They tell you what the power indicator is.

They tell you how it works.

They tell you why it is there.

Sometimes a heading can give you a clue about a word.

Look at these instructions.

WHAT TO DO IF YOUR TOASTER OVEN DOESN'T WORK

If your toaster oven malfunctions, call this toll-free number:

800-210-5531

We will tell you where to take your toaster oven for repairs.

You may not know the word "malfunctions."

But can you guess what it means?

Does the heading give you a clue?

The heading tells you what the instructions are about.

The instructions tell you what to do if your toaster oven doesn't work.

They tell you to call a number if your toaster oven <u>malfunctions</u>.

"Malfunctions" means "doesn't work."

The heading gives you a clue about the word.

———————————

A lot of instructions have words that you may not know.

But you can often use clues to guess what the words mean.

Sometimes a picture gives you a clue.

Sometimes the other words in the instructions give you a clue.

Sometimes a heading gives you a clue.

TRYING IT OUT

Read the instructions.

Then answer the questions about them.

CLEANING YOUR NEW COFFEE POT

Your new coffee pot is easy to clean.
Follow these three steps:

1. Unplug the coffee pot.
2. Use hot water and a soap pad to clean
   the inside of the pot.
3. Rinse out the inside of the pot with
   clean water and dry.

WARNING: Never put the base of your coffee pot
in water. Water will damage the base.

**NEVER IMMERSE
THE BASE IN WATER**

1. What are these instructions about?

2. What are the steps in the instructions for?

3. What should you use to clean the coffee pot?

4. What is the last step in cleaning the pot?

5. Look at the picture in the instructions.

   What does it show?

6. Look at the words under the picture.

   What does "immerse" mean?

   There are two clues to the meaning of "immerse."

   Can you find the clues?

Look at this label.

Then answer the questions about it.

DO-IT-ALL

BATHROOM CLEANER

WARNING: KEEP OUT
OF REACH OF CHILDREN.
DO-IT-ALL BATHROOM
CLEANER CONTAINS
TOXIC SUBSTANCES.

1. What is this label for?

2. What does the warning tell you?

3. Can you guess what "toxic substances" means?

    Are there any clues to help you guess?

4. What does the picture on the label tell you?

PUTTING WORDS IN THEIR PLACE

Fill in the blanks.

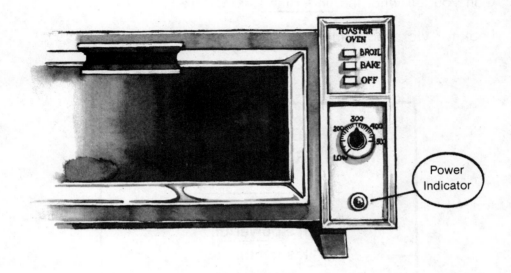

Your toaster oven comes with a power indicator.
The power indicator is a small light. When the
toaster oven is on, the power indicator lights up.
The power indicator will help you to use the toaster
oven safely. It will tell you when the toaster oven is on.

These instructions are for a toaster oven.

They tell you _____ the power indicator.

The _____ shows you the power indicator.

The _____ in the instructions _____ you

what the _____ indicator is.

LOOKING AT WORDS

Look at this ad.

Can you tell what the underlined words are?

Look for word parts that you know.

DO-IT-ALL
BATHROOM CLEANER

It's powerful.
It's useful.
It's helpful.
Try it.

TRYING IT ON YOUR OWN

Look for an instruction booklet.

Look for words you don't know.

Are there any clues to help you guess what the words are?

UNIT 8　　(REVIEW)

Read these instructions.

Then answer the questions about them.

DO-IT-ALL
RUG CLEANER

DIRECTIONS

 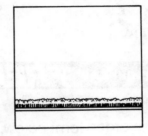 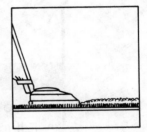

1. Hold spray can in an inverted position (top side down). Press button to spray cleaner onto rug.

2. Let cleaner stay on rug for 2 hours.

3. Remove cleaner from the rug with a vacuum cleaner. Your rug will look as good as new!

1. What are these instructions for?

2. What do the pictures in the instructions show?

3. How long should you let the cleaner stay on the rug?

4. What do the words "inverted position" mean? What clues tell you this?

Read this ad.

Then answer the questions about it on the next page.

1. What is this ad about?

2. What do you have to do to get a T-shirt?

3. What do you have to fill in on the order form?

4. Look at these lines from the order form:

   Children: S   M   L   XL

   Adult: S   M   L   XL

   What do the letters stand for?

   How can you tell?

Read these instructions.

Then answer the questions about them on the next page.

TESTING YOUR NEW SMOKE ALARM

Here's how to test your new smoke alarm to see if it works. First, get a 9-volt battery. Put it in place in the battery holder. The battery holder is at the back of the smoke alarm.

When the battery is in place, the alarm is ready to be tested. To test the alarm, press the <u>test button</u>. The test button is on the front of the alarm. Hold the test button down for 5–10 seconds. The alarm should go off.

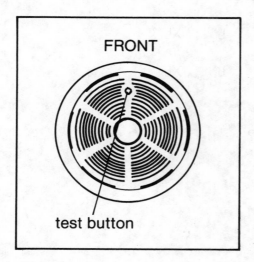

FRONT

test button

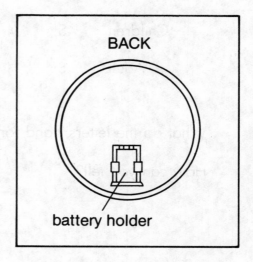

BACK

battery holder

If the alarm does not go off, try another 9-volt battery. If the alarm still does not go off, return the alarm to the store. It may be defective.

1. What are these instructions for?

2. What do the pictures in the instructions show?

3. You test the alarm.

   It doesn't go off.

   What should you do?

4. Look at the word "defective" in the last line.

   What does "defective" mean?

   How can you tell?

5. The steps for testing the smoke alarm are listed below.

   The steps are not in the right order.

   Put them in the right order.

   Press the test button.

   Put the battery in place in the battery holder.

   Get a 9-volt battery.

   Hold the test button down for 5–10 seconds.

Here is a table of contents.

Instruction booklet for

THE WORKSAVER

VACUUM CLEANER

About the Worksaver 2

How to clean rugs with the Worksaver 4

How to clean floors with the Worksaver 5

How to empty the Worksaver 7

How to get the Worksaver repaired 8

1. What booklet is this table of contents from?

2. What does the booklet tell you about?

3. You want to find out how to clean your floor with the Worksaver.
   What page in the booklet can help you?

4. Your Worksaver is not working.
   What page in the booklet tells you how to get it fixed?

Fill in the blanks.

TABLE OF CONTENTS

About your coffee maker .... page 3

How to use your coffee maker .... page 6

How to clean your coffee maker .... page 8

How to get new parts for your

                coffee maker .... page 11

Warranty information .... page 12

This is a _____ of contents.

A _____ of contents is a list of _____ .

There is a page _____ next to each _____ .

The page number _____ you where to _____ the

information you _____ .

Read the lines below.

The <u>underlined</u> word is made up of two short words.

Can you tell what the underlined words are?

June entered the Fud's Soda $25,000 <u>Giveaway</u>.

<u>However</u>, she didn't win anything.

<u>Someone</u> else won the $25,000.

The winner was Art <u>Drinkwater</u>.

UNIT 9

Suppose you wanted to find out the latest news.

What would you do?

You could watch a news show on TV.

You could listen to a news report on the radio.

The North Town News

serving North Town since 1926

Or you could read a newspaper.

A newspaper is one thing you can go to for the latest news.

A newspaper has all kinds of news in it.

It has news about things that are going on around the world.

It has news about things that are going on in the country.

It has news about things that are going on in your town.

Here are some of the things you may find in a newspaper.

IN TODAY'S PAPER:

World News 2
U.S. News 3
Local News 8
Business News 11
Sports 13

This list is part of an <u>index</u>.

A newspaper index is like a table of contents.

It gives you a list of headings.

The headings tell you the kinds of things that are in the
   newspaper.

The numbers next to the headings are page numbers.

They help you to find the things that are listed.

IN TODAY'S PAPER:

World News 2
U.S. News 3
Local News 8
Business News 11
Sports 13

How could you use the index to find something?

Suppose you wanted to find out the latest news about your town.

What page in the newspaper would you turn to?

You could look at the index to find out.

Look at the index at the top of this page.

One of the headings is "Local News."

"Local News" is news about the area you live in.

The index tells you that local news is on page 8.

You would turn to page 8 to find out what is happening in your town.

Here are some more headings from an index.

Movies/TV 15
Classified Ads 16
Obituaries 17
Editorial Page 24

These headings are for other things in a newspaper.

The first heading is "Movies/TV."

Most newspapers have a list of movies that are playing in your
     area.

Most newspapers have a list of shows that are on TV.

This heading tells you where to find these lists.

You can find them on page 15.

Movies/TV 15
Classified Ads 16
Obituaries 17
Editorial Page 24

The second heading is "Classified Ads."

Another name for "classified ads" is "want ads."

Jobs are listed in the want ads.

Used cars are listed in the want ads.

Houses and apartments are listed in the want ads.

The third heading in the index is "Obituaries."

Obituaries are death notices.

Most newspapers have an obituary page.

The last heading in the index is "Editorial Page."

Most newspapers have an editorial page.

There may be letters from readers on the editorial page.

The letters give the readers' feelings about the news.

The editorial page may also have an editorial on it.

The editorial gives the newspaper owner's feelings about the news.

———

Most newspapers are made up of many parts.

The parts are listed in the newspaper's index.

You can use the index to find out what the newspaper has in it.

You can use the index to find out where the parts are.

TRYING IT OUT

Here is an index from a newspaper.

Look at it.

Then answer the questions about it on the next page.

THE
WATERTOWN
DAILY NEWS

Index to Today's News:

World News 2

U.S. News 3

Local News 7

Editorials 11

Letters to the Editor 11

Sports 13

Business 17

Want Ads 19

Movies 23

TV Listings 24

Obituaries 25

1. What page would you turn to for the latest sports news?

2. You want to find out news about the Watertown area.

   What page would you turn to?

3. You want to find out what shows are on TV.

   What page would you turn to?

4. You are looking for a used car.

   You want to look at used car ads.

   What page would you turn to?

PUTTING WORDS IN THEIR PLACE

Fill in the blanks.

Use the words in the list.

IN TODAY'S PAPER:

World News 2
U.S. News 3
Local News 8
Business News 11
Sports 13

headings

page numbers

index

table of contents

newspaper

This list is part of a newspaper _____.

A newspaper index is like a _____.

A newspaper index is a list of _____.

The headings tell you the kinds of things that are in the

_____.

The numbers next to the headings are _____.

LOOKING AT WORDS

You looked at this line in this unit:

The editorial gives the newspaper <u>owner's</u> feelings about the news.

Look at the underlined word.

It is the word <u>owner</u> with <u>'s</u> added to it.

Whose feelings are given in the editorial?

They are the feelings of the newspaper owner.

They are the newspaper <u>owner's</u> feelings.

The <u>'s</u> shows who the feelings belong to.

TRYING IT ON YOUR OWN

Get a newspaper.

Look for an index to the newspaper.

What are the headings in the index?

Can you use the index to find things in the newspaper?

UNIT 10

What's the first thing you see when you look at a newspaper?

Most likely, the first thing you see is the front page headline.

In most newspapers, the most important news of the day is on the front page.

The biggest story of the day gets the biggest headline on the front page.

FIRE HITS DOWNTOWN AREA

Headlines are a very important part of a newspaper.

What is a headline?

What does it do?

A headline is the heading on a news story.

It tells you something about the main point of the story.

Headlines are easy to spot in a newspaper.

The letters that make up a headline are large.

Look at the headline at the top of this page.

Can you guess the main point of its story?

You can use headlines to find a story you want to read.

Suppose you want to find out about an election in your town.

You turn to the "Local News" page of the newspaper.

Local News

★ ★

MAYOR CALLS FOR MORE TAXES

McDonald Tops King in Local Election

DOWNTOWN FIRE BURNS OUT OF CONTROL FOR 3 HOURS

What's the quickest way to find the story?

The quickest way to find the story is to read the headlines.

Read each headline until you find the story you want to read.

Look at the headlines on page 90.

Which headline would be for the election story?

What might the other two headlines be for?

FIRE HITS DOWNTOWN AREA

**McDonald Tops
King in Local
Election**

Headlines are a very important part of a newspaper.

A headline is a heading on a news story.

It tells you something about the main point of the story.

You can find a story you want to read by reading the headlines.

TRYING IT OUT

Read these headlines.

Then answer the questions about them.

Food Prices Rise 5% in U.S.

CARDS BEAT BRAVES 4-2
AND MOVE INTO FIRST PLACE

TOWN WANTS MONEY TO FIX ROADS

1. Which headline would you find on the sports page?

2. Which headline is for a local news story?

3. Which headline would you find on the "U.S. News" page?

4. Do the headlines give you a clear idea about the stories?

PUTTING WORDS IN THEIR PLACE

Fill in the blanks.

This is a front page headline.

In most newspapers, the most _____ news of the day is

_____ the front page.

The biggest _____ story of the day gets _____ biggest headline.

Headlines are an _____ part of a newspaper.

A _____ tells you something about the _____ point of its story.

LOOKING AT WORDS

Read the lines below.

Some of the words are made up of two short words.

Can you find them?

There was a fire downtown the other day.

I read about it in the newspaper.

The story about the fire was on the front page.

There was a big headline above the story.

TRYING IT ON YOUR OWN

Get a newspaper.

Read the headlines.

Do the headlines give you an idea of what the stories are about?

UNIT 11

Reading a headline is a quick way to find out what a news story is about.

Most news headlines are very short.

Most headlines are only a few words long.

You looked at this headline in the last unit.

There are only four words in the headline.

But you can tell what the story is about from the headline.

The story is about a fire in the downtown area.

But look at this headline.

STATE EYES FED $

Do you have any idea what this headline means?

Can you guess what its story is about?

Some headlines look and sound strange.

The main reason for this is that headlines have to be short.

Headlines can't take up too much space on the page.

The people who make up the headlines have to take shortcuts.

Look at the headline again.

STATE EYES FED $

"State" means "the state government."

"Eyes" means "is looking for."

"Fed" is short for "federal."

It stands for the federal government.

"$" is a dollar sign.

It stands for money.

So what the headline means is this:

> The state government is looking for money from the federal
> government.

As you can see, some headlines are hard to understand.

It takes a lot of practice to figure out some headlines.

Look at this headline.

LOPEZ KO'S MERTZ

Can you figure out this headline?

You may have a hard time with this headline.

But you may find it easy to understand if you know the sport of
boxing.

This headline is about a boxing match.

"KO's" is short for "knocks out."

The headline tells you that Lopez knocked out Mertz in a boxing
match.

What should you do if you don't understand a headline?

The easiest thing to do is to read the first sentence of the story.

The first sentence usually tells you what the story is about.

Here is an example.

400 WORKERS AXED IN OK CUTBACK

In an effort to save money, the OK Food Company said yesterday that it is closing its Watertown plant and that the 400 workers in the plant would lose their jobs.

This story's headline may be hard to understand.

But the first sentence tells you what the story is about.

The OK Food Company is closing one of its plants.

Four hundred workers will lose their jobs.

The company is doing this to save money.

This is what the story is about.

Now look at the headline again.

Can you guess what "axed" means?

Can you guess what "cutback" means?

Reading a headline is a quick way to find out what a news story
is about.

But some headlines are hard to understand.

It takes a lot of practice to figure out some headlines.

If you don't understand a headline, read the first sentence of the
story.

The first sentence usually tells you what the story is about.

TRYING IT OUT

Read these headlines.

Can you figure out what the headlines are saying?

U.S. Jobless Rate at 8%

MAYOR: "WE'RE OUT OF CASH!"

Box Co. Nixes
Move to Westville

Here are the headlines from page 103.

Under each headline is the first sentence of the story.

Now can you tell what the stories are about?

Does the first sentence help you to understand the headline?

MAYOR: "WE'RE OUT OF CASH!"

Mayor Jane Short said today that North Town has run out of money.

U.S. Jobless Rate at 8%

The federal government reported today that 8% of the workers in the U.S. are out of work.

Box Co. Nixes Move to Westville

The Sunspot Box Company said today that it will not move its box-making plant to Westville.

PUTTING WORDS IN THEIR PLACE

The sentences below are about headlines.

Fill in the blanks.

Reading a headline is a quick way to find out what a news story
is about.

But most headlines are only _____ few words long.

Some headlines _____ hard to understand.

It takes a lot of practice to figure _____ some
headlines.

If you don't _____ a headline, read the first _____
of the story.

The first _____ usually tells you what the _____ is
about.

LOOKING AT WORDS

Look at these words.

        quick   quick<u>est</u>

        easy   easi<u>est</u>

The second word in each line is made up of two parts.

      quick + <u>est</u> ⟶ quickest

      easy + <u>est</u> ⟶ easiest

Read the lines below.

Look at the <u>underlined</u> words.

Can you tell what the underlined words are?

Some headlines are <u>harder</u> to understand than others.

Usually, the <u>longer</u> headlines are easier to understand.

The <u>shortest</u> headlines are usually the <u>hardest</u> to understand.

TRYING IT ON YOUR OWN

Look at the headlines in a newspaper.

Are any of the headlines hard to understand?

Does the first sentence in the story help you to understand the
    headline?

UNIT 12 (REVIEW)

Read these headlines.

Then answer the questions about them.

**New Report
Tells of Dangers
Of Smoking**

WORLD WAITS
FOR OUTCOME
OF U.S. ELECTION

Local Radio Station
Gets a New Owner

1. Which headline is for a local news story?

2. Which headline is for a world news story?

3. Look at the first headline.
   What do you think its story is about?

4. Look at the third headline.
   What does it tell you about the radio station?

Here is a newspaper index.

Look at it.

Then answer the questions about it on page 109.

NORTH TOWN NEWS

IN TODAY'S PAPER:

World News 2
U.S. News 3
Local News 8
Business News 11
Sports 13
Movies/TV 15
Classified Ads 16
Obituaries 17
Editorial Page 24

1. What newspaper is this index from?

2. On what page would you find business news?

3. On what page would you find death notices?

4. Suppose you want to find out what TV shows are on.

   What page would you turn to?

5. Suppose you want to read some news about North Town.

   What page would you turn to?

   Can you tell if there are any want ads in this paper?

Here is the front page of a newspaper.

Look at it.

Then answer the questions about it on page 111.

1. What is the name of the newspaper?

2. Which headline is about local food prices?

   What does it say about local food prices?

3. Can you tell which story is the biggest story of the day?

   How can you tell?

4. Which headline is about a food company?

   What did the food company do?

5. Which headline do you find hardest to understand?

Fill in the blanks.

Use the words in the list.

point
story
way
newspaper
heading

Headlines are a very important part of a _____ .

A headline is a _____ on a news story.

It tells you something about the main _____ of the story.

Reading a headline is a quick _____ to find out what a

news _____ is about.

The underlined words below are made up of two parts.

Draw a line between the two word parts.

Here are some examples.

Some head|lines are hard|er to under|stand than others.

There was a fire downtown the other day.

I read about the fire in the newspaper.

The story said it was one of the biggest fires ever in this town.

It said the fire started inside a food store.

UNIT 13

Here is a headline from a news story.

NORTH TOWN MAYOR QUITS!

Can you tell what this story is about?

The headline gives you a good clue.

The story is about the mayor of North Town.

The headline tells you that the mayor has quit.

Suppose you want to read this story.

You want to find out more about the mayor.

You read the first sentence of the story.

NORTH TOWN MAYOR QUITS!

Mayor Jane Short said today that she has resigned as mayor of North Town to start her own dry cleaning business.

The first sentence of this news story is long.

It is long because it is filled with <u>details</u>.

What are <u>details</u>?

Details are the facts that make up a story.

NORTH TOWN MAYOR QUITS!

Mayor Jane Short said today that she
has resigned as mayor of North Town
to start her own dry cleaning business.

The first sentence in most news stories is long.

Sometimes a long sentence is hard to understand.

But there is a way to make a long sentence easier to understand.

Try to read the sentence in <u>parts</u>.

Think about what each part says.

After you read all the parts, put them together.

Think about what the whole sentence says.

Here is an example of how to read a sentence in parts.

   Mayor Jane Short said today

   that she has resigned as mayor of North Town

   to start her own dry cleaning business.

Look at the parts of this sentence.

The first part tells you who the story is about.

The second part tells you what happened.

The third part tells you why it happened.

Mayor Jane Short said today

that she has resigned as mayor of North Town

to start her own dry cleaning business.

When you know the details, you can put them together.

You can make it easier to understand the story.

The story is telling you that Mayor Jane Short has quit.

She has quit to start her own dry cleaning business.

Here is another long sentence from a news story.

Try to read it in parts.

Report Says
High Prices
Keep People
At Home

A report from the
federal government
shows that, because of
the high cost of living,
fewer people are going
to the movies.

What are the parts of the sentence?

Here is the first part.

A report from the federal government shows that

This part tells you what the story is about.

It is about a report.

Here is the second part.

because of the high cost of living

This part gives you a reason for something.

Here is the third part.

fewer people are going to the movies.

This part tells you what the report said.

After you know the details, you can put them together.

You can understand the sentence.

A government report says that
fewer people are going to the movies
because of the high cost of living.

_____

Sometimes a long sentence is hard to understand.

But there is a way to make a long sentence easier to understand.

Try to read the sentence in parts.

Think about the details in each part.

Then put the parts together.

TRYING IT OUT

Here are some sentences from news stories.

Try to read them in parts.

Then answer the questions about them.

WXXA, the Watertown
area's only radio station, is
being sold to a group of
local businesses headed by
the OK Food Company.

1. What is WXXA?

2. What is happening to WXXA?

3. Who is buying WXXA?

4. What would be a good headline for this story?

**Westville police said today
that two men armed with
machine guns walked into the
Burger Heaven store on East
Road and took $325 in cash.**

1. What did the two men have with them?

2. Where did the two men go?

3. What did they take?

4. On what road is the Burger Heaven store?

5. Who gave the report about the two men?

6. What would be a good headline for this story?

The head of the North
Town Fire Department
said today that last week's
fire in the downtown area
started because of a
defective light switch in
the North Town Food
Store.

1. Who gave the report about the fire?

2. When did the fire happen?

3. Where did the fire happen?

4. Why did the fire happen?

5. Where did the fire start?

6. What would be a good headline for this story?

PUTTING WORDS IN THEIR PLACE

Fill in the blanks.

Mayor Jane Short said today
that she has resigned as mayor of
North Town to start her own
dry cleaning business.

This story is about the mayor of _____ .

The mayor's name is _____ .

The mayor said that she has _____ .

She wants to start her own _____ business.

LOOKING AT WORDS

Look at the underlined words in the lines below.

Each underlined word is made up of two word parts.

You have looked at one of the parts in this unit.

Can you tell what the underlined words are?

Our state has a new governor.

He used to be a businessman.

He used to own a lighting company.

He seems to be a reasonable person.

I hope he does a good job governing the state.

TRYING IT ON YOUR OWN

Look at the first sentences in news stories.

Are they long?

Try to read the long sentences in parts.

Are they easier to understand?

UNIT 14

Look at this headline.

**BOX COMPANY
REACHES ACCORD
WITH WORKERS**

What does "accord" mean?

You may not have ever seen the word "accord."

It's not a word that you see every day.

Are there any clues in the headline to help you with the word?

There aren't any good clues in the headline.

But look at the first sentence of the story.

BOX COMPANY REACHES ACCORD WITH WORKERS

The Sunspot Box Company has reached an agreement with its 750 workers that will give each worker a 9% pay raise.

Now can you tell what "accord" means?

The sentence says that the company has reached an agreement with the workers.

The headline says "BOX COMPANY REACHES ACCORD WITH WORKERS."

An accord is an agreement.

The sentence gives you a clue about what the word "accord" means in the headline.

Here is another news story.

Read the headline and the first sentence.

Then answer the questions.

Mayor Queries Governor on Sales Tax Rise

Mayor Billy Goodman of Westville today asked Governor Sid Allwell about the governor's plans to increase the state's sales tax to 8%.

What is this story about?

What did the mayor ask the governor about?

Look at the headline.

What does the word "queries" mean?

How can you tell?

Mayor Queries Governor on Sales Tax Rise

Mayor Billy Goodman
of Westville today
asked Governor Sid
Allwell about the
governor's plans to
increase the state's
sales tax to 8%.

The sentence gives you a clue about the word "queries."

The headline says that the mayor queried the governor.

The first sentence in the story says that the mayor asked the
governor.

Queries means asks.

_____

Sometimes the headline can give you a clue about a word in the
story.

Look at the headline and story on the next page.

NEW MAYOR SAYS
HIS FIRST JOB
IS TO GET MONEY

Fred Price, the new
mayor of North Town,
said today that his
initial job as North
Town's mayor is to get
more tax money for the
town from the state.

Look at the word "initial" in the story.

You may not know what the word means in the story.

But the headline gives you a clue.

The headline tells you about the mayor's <u>first</u> job.

The story tells you about his <u>initial</u> job.

In the story, <u>initial</u> means <u>first</u>.

**BOX COMPANY
REACHES ACCORD
WITH WORKERS**

---

*Mayor Queries
Governor on
Sales Tax Rise*

You may not know every word in a headline or a news story.

But sometimes you can use clues to find out what a word means.

Sometimes the story gives you a clue about a word in the headline.

Sometimes the headline gives you a clue about a word in the story.

TRYING IT OUT

Read the headline and the story.

Then answer the questions.

Company Tells Workers Their Jobs Are Safe

The Sunspot Box Company today informed the 750 workers at its plant in Goodland that the company will not move the plant to a new area and that the workers will not lose their jobs.

1. What is this story about?

2. What did the workers find out about their jobs?

3. Find the word <u>informed</u> in the story.

   Can you tell what <u>informed</u> means?

   Does the headline give you a clue?

Here is a sports story.

Braves Throttle Cards, 7–1, In Crucial Ball Game

Tom Waterhouse had four hits
and Ed Forman had three hits as
the Braves beat the Cards, 7–1, in
an important baseball game last
night.

1. What is this story about?

2. How many hits did Ed Forman have?

3. Look at the word <u>throttle</u> in the headline.

    Does the story give you a clue about the meaning of <u>throttle</u>?

    What is the clue?

4. Look at the word <u>crucial</u> in the headline.

    Does the story give you a clue about the meaning of <u>crucial</u>?

    What is the clue?

PUTTING WORDS IN THEIR PLACE

Fill in the blanks.

BOX COMPANY
REACHES ACCORD
WITH WORKERS

The Sunspot Box
Company has reached an
agreement with its 750
workers that will give
each worker a 9% pay
raise.

This story is about the Sunspot _____ Company.

The company has _____ an agreement with its workers.

The agreement gives each _____ a 9% pay raise.

The word <u>accord</u> in the headline means _____ .

There are 750 _____ at the box company.

LOOKING AT WORDS

Look at the underlined words in the lines below.

Each underlined word is made up of two word parts.

You have looked at one of the parts in this unit.

Can you tell what the underlined words are?

Ed was telling me about his newest job.

He said he is having a hard time with the job.

He said the job is giving him a headache.

He is finding out that he doesn't like the job.

UNIT 15   (REVIEW)

You have looked at some important things in this book.

First, you looked at instructions.

Reading instructions is important in everyday life.

A lot of things that you read are instructions.

Second, you looked at some parts of the newspaper.

You looked at the newspaper's index.

You looked at a news story's headlines and first sentence.

You also looked at some clues to reading instructions and the newspaper.

The clues can help make reading easier for you.

There are some instructions and news stories to read on the next few pages.

There are also some questions about them.

Use the clues you have looked at to answer the questions.

Here are some instructions.

DO-IT-ALL
SPRAY CLEANER

makes cleaning your windows
as EASY as 1–2–3!

1   2   3

1. Hold bottle in the upright position (top side up).
   Point spray nozzle away from you.

2. Point spray nozzle at window and press down.

3. Wipe cleaner from window. Your window will
   look cleaner than ever!

1. What are these instructions for?

2. What do the pictures in the instructions show?

3. What does the arrow in the first picture show?

4. What do the words "upright position" mean?
   What clues tell you this?

Here are some more instructions.

OK
PEA SOUP
MIX

Cooking Directions:

1. Boil 1 cup of water.
2. Empty 1 pack of
   OK INSTANT PEA SOUP
   into a coffee cup.
3. Pour boiling water
   into the cup.
4. Stir the soup for 15
   seconds. Your soup
   is ready to eat!

1. What do these instructions tell you about?

2. What is the first thing to do in the instructions?

3. What is the last thing to do?

4. How much soup can you make with one pack of this soup mix?
   How can you tell?

Here is a table of contents.

Instruction Booklet for

THE LIFE SAVER
SMOKE ALARM

About your new smoke alarm .... page 3

Setting up your new smoke alarm .... page 4

Where is the best place to put a smoke alarm? .... page 5

Testing your new smoke alarm .... page 7

What to do if your smoke alarm doesn't work .... page 8

1. What kind of booklet is this table of contents for?

2. On what page could you find out how to set up the smoke
    alarm?

3. On what page could you find out how to test the smoke
    alarm?

4. Suppose you test the smoke alarm and it doesn't work.
    On what page could you find out what to do next?

Here is an index from a newspaper.

THE
WESTVILLE
POST

In today's paper:

HEADLINES FROM AROUND
    THE WORLD 3
HEADLINES FROM THE U.S. 7
WESTVILLE AREA NEWS 11
THE POST EDITORIALS 13
OBITUARIES 14
SPORTS 15
CLASSIFIEDS 19
TV/MOVIE LISTINGS 28

1. What newspaper is this index from?

2. What page in the newspaper would you turn to for world news headlines?

3. What page would you turn to for sports news?

4. What page would you turn to for local news?

5. You want to look at the want ads.
   Can you tell if this paper has want ads?
   How can you tell?

Here is a page from a newspaper.

Answer the questions about it on page 143.

THE WATERTOWN DAILY NEWS

25¢

★ ★ ★ ★

STATE SALES TAX HITS 8%

Governor Gets His Way

State to Use Sales Tax $ To Fix Roads

SHOW BIZ KING HITS THE SKIDS

U.S. JOBLESS RATE NOW AT 8.3%

World Gas Prices On Rise Again

1. What is the name of this newspaper?

2. Do you think this is the front page of the newspaper?

3. What story is the biggest story of the day?

4. How many headlines are about the state sales tax?

5. Which headline is about world gas prices?

   What does it say about world gas prices?

6. Look at this headline:

   U.S. JOBLESS RATE NOW AT 8.3%

   What do you think this headline means?

Here is a news story.

Company Announces
Power Plant Shutdown

The Outwater Power and
Light Company said today
that it will close down its
Watertown power plant next
month because the plant costs
too much money to run.

1. What is going to happen to the Watertown power plant?

2. Why is it going to happen?

3. When is it going to happen?

4. Look at the word "shutdown" in the headline.
   What does it mean?

5. What do you think the Outwater Power Company has to do
   with the power plant?

Here is another news story.

STATE GOV'T TO LOOK INTO NORTH TOWN'S $ WOES

Mayor Fred Price of
North Town said
today that the
state government
will conduct an
investigation to find
out why North Town
has run out of money.

1. What did the mayor say?

2. What is the mayor's name?

3. Look at this sentence part:

    the state government will <u>conduct an investigation</u>

    What does "conduct an investigation" mean?
    Does the headline give you a clue?

4. Look at the word "gov't" in the headline.
   What does it stand for?

Here is another news story.

COMPANY HONCHO
GETS 2 DAYS

The head of the Fud's
Soda Company was
sentenced today to 2
days in jail for hitting
a policeman who had
given him a speeding
ticket.

1. Look at the word "honcho" in the headline.

    What does it mean?

    Does the first sentence of the story give you a clue?

2. What happened to the head of the Fud's Soda Company?

3. Why did it happen?

4. Does the headline give you a good idea about what is in the story?

APPENDIX: Unit Outlines and Word Lists

This book is a guide to reading. To be most effective, the material presented in this book should be supplemented by material that a student may encounter in everyday life. The student should take the points raised in this book and see how they apply in the real world. In this way, the strategies and skills that are pointed out in this book will not be learned in a vacuum.

On the following pages, you will find a rough outline for each unit in this book (with the exception of the review units). The outlines contain the following information:

- general objective of the unit
- a list of new words used in the unit
- the total number of different words used in the unit
- suggested preview activities
- suggested post-unit activities

You can use this information any way you choose. You can use it to supplement an existing lesson plan, or you can use it as an outline for a lesson plan. You may want to revise or recast the suggested activities to fit the special interests or needs of students. The most important thing to do is to place the material in this book within the context of the student's experiences and expectations. Get the student to relate the things in this book to what he may see in the course of a day. Have the student apply the strategies and skills to things that he wants to read. A student will come to understand more about reading by looking at things that interest him rather than by practicing skills and strategies only within the context of a single book.

A NOTE ABOUT THE WORD LISTS

New words that are introduced in a unit appear in the word list for that unit. The words listed for Unit 1 are words that do not appear in Book 1 of Living in the Reader's World. There are only two kinds of words that are not listed in the word lists: proper names and difficult words that are used only to get the student to use context clues to infer their meaning. Nouns and verbs that have their plurals or singulars formed by adding s are listed only once.

UNIT 1 (pages 1–10)

Objective: The student is introduced to examples of instructions and analyzes them for meaning.

Number of different words used in unit: 160

Number of new words used in unit: 52

WORD LIST

adults	doctor	machine	station
ages	doesn't	money	tablet(s)
alarm	door	or	than
aspirin	dosage	passing	there's
bottle	empty	pets	thumb
bottle's	enter	press	tone
button	every	pull	waiting
by	handle	push	warning
cap	headache	quarters	will
case	instructions	reach	work(s)
children	isn't	safe	yield
deposit	keep	see	younger
dial	label	smoking	you're

Preview activities: Ask students if they can think of the last time they either gave or received instructions. What were the instructions for? Why were they necessary? Did the instructions help the person to understand something better? Then talk about instructions that appear in print. Ask students if they can think of any instructions that they might read during the course of a day.

Post-unit activities: Ask students to look for an example of some type of written instructions. Have the students bring in the instructions (if possible) to discuss them.

UNIT 2   (pages 11–19)

Objective: The student looks at the steps in instructions and sees the importance of sequence to instructions.

Number of different words used in unit: 141

Number of new words used in unit: 31

address	dialing	heat	pot
again	didn't	I	started
appear	directions	into	step(s)
aren't	first	listened	still
boiling	follow	nothing	wasn't
bottom	form	OK	water
deposited	given	opening	working
desired	happened	pay	

<u>Preview activities</u>: Discuss with students the point that many instructions are given in steps. Use as an example a hypothetical situation in which someone needs directions to get to a certain place. Does the person need to follow each step in the right order to get to the place?

<u>Post-unit activities</u>: Ask students to bring in any example of instructions from a package of food. Are the steps put in a specific order? Are they separated visually from one another? Does a person need to follow the exact order of the steps to prepare the food properly?

UNIT 3   (pages 20–32)

<u>Objective</u>: The student looks at how a heading can be used to find instructions.

<u>Number of different words used in unit</u>: 124

<u>Number of new words used in unit</u>: 22

WORD LIST

card	emptied	ingredients	toll
code	followed	making	wanted
coin	found	never	which
collect	had	oz.	you've
credit	heated	slot	
distance	information	stock	

<u>Preview activities</u>: Find a product label (such as a label from a soup can) on which directions for using the product appear along with other kinds of information about the product, and show the label to students. Ask students to think of the fastest way to find the directions among the other pieces of information. Discuss the point that headings can be used to locate the directions easily and quickly.

<u>Post-unit activities</u>: Discuss with students the point that headings are often used on labels, in instruction booklets, in newspapers, etc. Discuss the idea that headings tell a person what kind of information is given. Ask students to discuss the helpfulness of headings in reading.

UNIT 5   (pages 37–47)

Objective: The student looks at how headings are organized in a table of contents; the student also looks at how illustrations may be used to make instructions easier to understand.

Number of different words used in unit: 164

Number of new words used in unit: 35

WORD LIST

anything	full	maker	slide
booklet(s)	glass	minutes	so
box	holder	my	someday
brew	hole	outside	switch
clean	hope	plug	table
cold	however	pour	try
contents	I'll	ready	unit
everything	inside	scoop	whatever
filter	its	set	

Preview activities: Ask students to imagine that they have just bought a new appliance, one that they have never used before. How would they find out how to use it? Discuss the point that many home appliances come with instruction booklets that explain what the appliance is and how it should be used.

UNIT 6   (pages 48–59)

Objective: The student looks at how diagrams and pictures can help explain instructions that may be difficult to understand.

Number of different words used in unit: 157

Number of new words used in unit: 34

WORD LIST

air	clearer	onto	test
attach	dots	people	tested
bath	fast	return	testing
battery	front	room	thinker
bedroom	got	saver	volt
best	inches	screws	waiter
boxer	kitchen	setting	wall
bracket	living	snap	worker
ceiling	often		

Preview activities: Discuss with students the idea that pictures are often used to make a point clearer. You may want to give examples of advertisements in which pictures help to illustrate the idea of the ad.

Post-unit activities: Ask students to look for examples of illustrated instructions and to bring them in for discussion.

UNIT 7   (pages 60–68)

Objective: The student uses such context clues as pictures, headings, and familiar words to determine the meanings of unfamiliar words in instructions.

Number of different words used in unit: 129

Number of new words used in unit: 20

WORD LIST

base	damage	pad	seen
bathroom	dry	power	small
cleaner	hot	powerful	toaster
cleaning	light(s)	repairs	unplug
contains	oven	rinse	useful

Preview activities: Review the use of headings and pictures in instructions. How do they make the instructions easier to understand? Have students refer back to the instructions on page 40. Ask them to imagine that they did not know the names of the parts of the coffee maker. Are there any clues in the pictures to help them figure out what the names of the parts were?

Post-unit activities: Discuss with students the point that many instruction booklets and similar kinds of reading material contain technical words or language that most people do not understand easily. Discuss the idea that pictures, diagrams, arrows, etc., are often used to make technical words or language more understandable.

UNIT 9   (pages 77–87)

Objective: The student looks at how a newspaper's index functions as a sort of table of contents for the newspaper; the student also looks at some common features of a newspaper.

Number of different words used in unit: 143

Number of new words used in unit: 31

WORD LIST

apartments	daily	latest	playing
area	death	local	reader(s)
around	editor	obituaries	readers'
belong	editorial(s)	obituary	report
business	feelings	owner	sports
car(s)	happening	owner's	watch
classified	index	paper	whose
country	jobs	person	

<u>Preview activities</u>: Have students discuss their feelings about news. Do they think that knowing the latest news is important? How do they find out the latest news? Is there any specific kind of news (such as sports, politics, etc.) that is of special interest to them? (Note: In this unit, some specialized new terms (<u>classified ads</u>, <u>editorials</u>, and <u>obituaries</u>) are used. You may want to preview these terms for the students before beginning the unit.)

UNIT 10   (pages 88–95)

<u>Objective</u>: The student looks at headlines (headings of new stories) to determine the main point of a story.

<u>Number of different words used in unit</u>: 115

<u>Number of new words used in unit</u>: 16

WORD LIST

biggest	fix	might	spot
clear	headline(s)	move	stories
downtown	hits	quickest	story
election	likely	rise	very

<u>Preview activities</u>: Review with students the ways in which headings are used in instructions and in a news index. Then point out the fact that news stories usually have headings. Look at some front-page headlines with the students. Read the headlines. Do the headlines give an idea of what the stories are about?

<u>Post-unit activities</u>: Select some news stories from a local newspaper. Ask students to read the headlines on the stories. Then ask them if they can tell what the stories are about. You may also ask them to identify where the story might be found in the newspaper (i.e., in the local news section, in the sports section, etc.).

UNIT 11 (pages 96–106)

Objective: The student uses the first sentence of a news story to determine the meaning of unfamiliar words in a headline.

Number of different words used in unit: 172

Number of new words used in unit: 34

WORD LIST

boxing	few	lose	shortest
cash	figure	mayor	space
cuts	government	plant(s)	story's
doing	harder	practice	strange
dollar	hardest	quick	too
easiest	jobless	reported	usually
effort	knocked	run	we're
eyes	knocks	saying	yesterday
federal	longer		

Preview activities: In this unit, students will be dealing with some unfamiliar words and abbreviated grammatical structures that are a part of newspaper headline "language." As an introduction to this unit, discuss with students the idea that people have invented many specialized "languages" that may be hard to understand at first. Point out examples of specialized vocabulary used in sports (first down, double play, etc.), cooking (over easy, deep fry, etc.), weather reports (cold front, high pressure, etc.), and the like. Ask students if they are familiar with a specialized "language" that other people may find hard to understand.

Post-unit activities: Ask students to find examples of newspaper headlines that are hard to understand. Ask them to look at the first sentence of the story to see if the first sentence helps them to understand what the story is about and what the headline means.

UNIT 13 (pages 114–126)

Objective: The student looks at longer sentences from news stories; the student works on reading a longer sentence in parts in order to understand the sentence better.

Number of different words used in unit: 181

Number of new words used in unit: 26

WORD LIST

area's	facts	headed	reasonable
armed	fewer	high	resigned
being	filled	lighting	seems
businessman	governing	mayor's	sold
buying	governor	men	telling
cost	guns	quit(s)	walked
details	head		

Preview activities: Review the point that instructions are often divided into steps or parts in order to make them easier to understand. Have students look at some of the first sentences of news stories. Discuss the point that most first sentences of news stories are very long and filled with details.

Post-unit activities: Have students work with news stories from a local newspaper to practice reading longer sentences.

UNIT 14   (pages 127–136)

Objective: The student uses the context of familiar words to determine the meaning of unfamiliar words in news stories.

Number of different words used in unit: 144

Number of new words used in unit: 17

WORD LIST

agreement	governor's	mayor's	plans
asked	him	me	reached
ball	his	newest	state's
ever	increase	night	tax
giving			

Preview activities: Review the points covered in Unit 7 of this book.

Post-unit activities: Have students look at headlines in a newspaper to find words that they do not recognize. Are there any clues in the story that can help them to guess at the meaning of the unfamiliar words? Are there any other clues (such as photographs) that may be of some help?